# G ORWELL

# AT THE BBC IN 1942

**FINDING OUT HOW TO SET FREE HIS GENIUS**

## Desmond Avery

*with Preface by Tim Crook*

THE GARTH PRESS

ISBN 978-1-9997307-0-3

The author thanks the Orwell Society
(www.orwellsociety.com, info@orwellsociety.com) for
publishing an earlier version of this study in instalments on
its web site, and Kathryn Hughes for much valuable advice
on how to explore this subject in the first place.

Published by The Garth Press, Wellingore

Printed and bound in the UK by:
Witley Press Ltd, Hunstanton, Norfolk
www.witleypress.co.uk

# Contents

# Preface

Desmond Avery joins Professor Peter Davison and myself in a growing number of George Orwell scholars who do not believe his time at the BBC during the Second World War were 'two wasted years'.

The BBC now acknowledges this to the extent that they are hosting a bronze statue of Orwell by Martin Jennings in front of their new Broadcasting House. The Orwell maxim 'If liberty means anything at all, it means the right to tell people what they do not want to hear' will be inscribed upon the wall behind. Jennings depicts the author: 'loomingly tall, skinny as a rake, forever fag in hand, body leaning in to make a point. He wore the kind of clothes that might have spent their off-duty hours hanging from a nail in the potting shed.'

In this enlightening and brilliant study, Avery has appreciated how the discipline, culture and context of those years as a Talks Producer in the

BBC's Eastern Service provided Orwell with significant writing development and confidence. They were transformative. His two essays 'Politics and the English Language' and 'Poetry and the Microphone' express the degree to which his creative, political and intellectual imagination was intensified by broadcasting, producing propaganda and cultural programming. Political writing and art sparked into a devastating fusion which gestated *Animal Farm* and *Nineteen Eighty-Four*. This book explains how that happened.

One intriguing question worth asking is who exactly did the BBC employ? Was it George Orwell, or Eric Arthur Blair? Biographers and scholars of George Orwell Studies are becoming increasingly focused on the bifurcation between the two personas. While Orwell's boss at the BBC left high praise for his service in the Corporation's archives, others have observed that Eric Arthur Blair could be egotistic and awkward.

It is certainly ironic that however inept Mr. Blair was in his day-to-day dealings with colleagues, the release to the National Archives of his MI5 and Special Branch files prove that he was under surveillance. And the informants quite possibly included left-wing and progressive Indian intellectuals working in the BBC whose cause of self-determination and eventual independence Orwell was emphatically in favour of. The Big Brother State was watching George Orwell.

Orwell was generally rather negative when he reflected on his BBC experience. Six months in he compared it to a girls' school and lunatic asylum. Later he would talk about the moral squalor, ultimate futility, and frustration of broadcasting at that time. But Orwell had a full grasp of double-think, and Avery recognizes that his phlegmatic and self-deprecatory observations about working in the BBC did have an 'on the other hand' perspective.

He saw the value and importance of English language and literature as a weapon of war. It is also clear that Orwell had a fundamental understanding of the romance and art of broadcasting. In the first edition of his arts programme *Voice* he seemed to relish the idea that radio waves travel on endlessly and should be audible in the great nebula Orion nearly a million years hence.

Orwell fashioned a literary aesthetic out of oscillating between pessimism and optimism. His writing bounced mischievously between joy and despair and that reflects the tone of his BBC experience. One day he would be raging that his broadcasts were useless because nobody was listening. On another he would be engaging T.S. Eliot to read his poetry, or dramatizing an imaginative interview with his hero Jonathan Swift.

*George Orwell at the BBC in 1942* is an excellent read for anyone wanting to fully appreciate how a radio broadcasting career, albeit for only around two years, laid the foundations for the creation of two of the most influential books in 20th century English literature.

TIM CROOK

# Introduction and up to 1941

'I have left the BBC after two wasted years in it and have become literary editor of the Tribune, a leftwing weekly which you may have seen. It leaves me a little spare time, which the BBC didn't, so I have got another book under weigh [sic],' George Orwell wrote from London to Philip Rahv in New York in December 1943.[1]

The book was *Animal Farm*. He could have started on it sooner if he had not been so busy organizing radio programmes, but then could he have done it quite so well, and with such perfect disillusionment? After that came *Nineteen Eighty-Four*, which drew so heavily on the BBC experience that it could not have been written at all without it. So Orwell's opinion that those two

---

[1] Letter to Philip Rahv, 9 December 1943. In: Peter Davison, ed., *The Complete Works of George Orwell, Vol. XVI, I Have Tried to Tell the Truth.* London: Secker & Warburg, 1998; p. 22.

years were wasted is questionable. He joined the staff on 18 August 1941 and left on 24 November 1943 and by that time, one could argue, he had learnt what he needed to know to write the two books that have made him a giant. To try for a more accurate idea of how he spent that part of his life I will focus on 1942 because it contains a full range of his work as well as his transition from beginner in broadcasting to seasoned practitioner. It was also the year in which he turned 39, the same age as Winston Smith in 1984, his imagined 'last man in Europe'. Churchill's book about the Second World War covering 1942 is called *The Hinge of Fate* because that year determined the outcome of the war. It can be seen as the hinge of Orwell's fate as a writer as well.

His biographers take his word for it, and inform us that the BBC work was a waste of time. Bernard Crick writes in 1980: 'Then for two precious years his talents were mainly wasted, his colleagues later agreed, in producing cultural programmes for intellectuals in India and South-East Asia, heard by few and unlikely to have influenced even them.'[2] D. J. Taylor sees it the

---

[2] Bernard Crick, *George Orwell: A Life*. London: Penguin, 1980, p. 413.

same way in 2003: 'There was no let-up in Orwell's work-rate – the scripts for news commentaries, educational talks and drama adaptations continued to pour forth – but he was conscious that he was wasting his time.'[3] The fewness of his listeners and the lowness of his audience approval ratings prove it, both authorities explain. It implies that if he had become a radio celebrity of that era, like J. B. Priestley for example, he would have been spending his time well, but that too is questionable.

In January 2011, however, Peter Davison, editor of the 20-volume *Complete Works*, argued that the BBC time was far from wasted, drawing attention to the many valuable programmes Orwell made, showing how listeners and the Corporation itself did in fact benefit from them much more than is usually assumed.[4] It is a point well worth making but still leaves intact the verdict of Crick and Taylor, and that of George

---

[3] D. J. Taylor, *Orwell: The Life*. London: Vintage, 2003, p. 323. Gordon Bowker, in *George Orwell* (London: Little Brown, 2003, pp. 291-2), is more tentative but does not explore the issue.

[4] Peter Davison, 'Two Wasted Years?' *Finlay Publisher – The Orwell Essay*, 2011, January – March, accessed at www.finlay-publisher.com on 12 April 2011.

Woodcock, Orwell's anarchist friend, who said: 'I know he managed to introduce one or two astonishing items in his broadcasts, but he soon found there was in fact little he could do, and he left the BBC in disgust.'[5]

If he had spent those two of his nine remaining years of life on 'real writing', we might still want to imagine, he could have gone even further, and perhaps fitted in another masterpiece or two before he died. That may be how he himself felt about it at the time, and saying so would have reassured his left-wing friends that he disapproved of the British establishment and its voice. But for us now to agree with him would be to leave unexamined the leap in quality from, say, *Coming Up for Air* in 1939, his most successful piece of fiction up till then, and the next one, *Animal Farm*, in 1945. The former was amusing and perhaps mildly disturbing at best, whereas the latter is a book which, to use Orwell's own expression, changed the world.

A surge in a writer's power must always have some causes that cannot be known, but in this case there are quite a few that can be. From 1941 to

---

[5] Quoted by Crick, p. 418, from George Woodcock, *The Writer and Politics*. London: Porcupine Press, 1948.

1943 the writer in question was acquiring mass communication skills in a medium that was new to him, keeping track of events and trying to influence them during a critical time in history, delving into the riches of English literature for an international audience, fitting in with other people's plans and priorities, listening to the competition, making himself as interesting and convincing as he possibly could for a sceptical audience, and in general getting cured of some of the comparatively ineffective writing habits he had had before. Writers with real ambitions would pay for such a drastic retraining regime. He was being paid to do it, at the starting rate of £640 a year with an annual increment of £40,[6] which made it worthwhile for him materially, as well as professionally.

His novels up till this watershed in his writing life expressed disgust at the status quo, frustration at the apparent impossibility of changing it, and consequent self-disgust. They heaped scorn on existing people and institutions in potentially actionable ways which routinely put his first publisher, Victor Gollancz, into a state of extreme

---

[6] Contract dated 18 August 1941. *Works, vol. XIII, All Propaganda is Lies*, p. 4.

anxiety. They were also weakly plotted and contained two-dimensional characters, unsolved problems and improbable events. *Coming Up for Air*, published in 1939, achieved a new kind of fluency by using the device of a deliberately ridiculous first-person narrator, but it failed to produce even one convincing character or any enduringly strong sensation or idea. It just stuck to the story he had told in all his novels, of an antihero who failed, with an insipid sense of futility and embarrassment rather than tragedy. Perhaps that was his version of the truth about life, and he never abandoned it, but at least later he acquired a much stronger sense of how unsatisfactory it was. None of his fiction was short of insights or emotions, but he never found a way to engage them fully in conventional novel-writing. More promising approaches did not occur to him until his wartime job disrupted these routines.

He set out his wartime hopes and plans at the beginning of 1940 in a letter to Geoffrey Gorer:

I have so far completely failed to serve HM. government in any capacity, though I want to, because it seems to me that now we are in this bloody war we have got to win it & I would like to lend a hand. They won't have me in the army, at any rate at present, because of my lungs. Eileen has got a job in a government department, which as usual she got by knowing somebody who knew somebody, etc., etc. I also want a job because I want to lay off writing for a bit, I feel I have written myself out and ought to lie fallow. I am sort of incubating an enormous novel, the family saga sort of thing, only I don't want to begin it before I'm all set.[7]

It's hard to imagine what a successful enormous novel by Orwell could have been like, but his sense of the potential for improvement is a good sign. There was a new relaxed narrative ease in *Coming up for Air*, and an entirely new depth of conviction in *Homage to Catalonia*. He must have been aware that the two could be combined somehow. Meanwhile, to keep earning a living, he took on as much freelance journalism as he could manage, which included some broadcasting. The latter led eventually to his joining the Eastern Service of the BBC's Empire Department as a Talks Assistant – later 'Producer, Indian Section'

---

[7] Letter to Geoffrey Gorer, 10 January 1940. In Peter Davison, ed. *Orwell: A Life in Letters*. London: Harvill Secker, 2010; p. 174.

– on 18 August 1941. With Japan's abrupt entry and rapid progress in the war, the BBC was scrambling to build up its propaganda offensive in the East and keep the colonies on side.

Orwell had also joined the Home Guard as soon as it was formed, and served as platoon commander in the St John's Wood Company where he was known as Sergeant Blair. In that role he struck his second publisher and fellow volunteer, Fredric Warburg, a First World War veteran, as 'austere, resolute, implacably determined to destroy his enemies without fear or mercy, if only they came within his reach.'[8] His wife of six years, Eileen, like Winston Smith, worked in the Censorship Department at the Ministry of Information – 'daily work of inconceivable dullness,' she called it,[9] and transferred in the spring of 1942 to the Ministry of Food. It was an improvement but she continued to suffer from poor health and depression. At that time Orwell was known mainly for his socialist and patriotic beliefs as expressed in polemical journalism and essays, especially *The Road to*

[8] Fredrick Warburg, *All Authors are Equal*. London: Hutchinson, 1973; p. 36.

[9] Letter from Eileen Blair to Norah Myles, March 1941. Included in Letters, p. 188.

*Wigan Pier*, his first big seller, and as an interesting but patchy novelist.

His BBC responsibilities included writing at least one weekly news summary – a ten-minute account of what had happened in the war during the past week aimed at inspiring support for the Allied cause. It amounted to direct propaganda and was accompanied by indirect kinds in the form of cultural and educational programmes mainly on English literature. In addition, he continued to write articles for print, and kept a sporadic diary. His work during that time thus shows a full spectrum of his thinking, from publicly official to privately anti-official. His occasional articles for print probably received his most sustained intellectual engagement, but as he gets used to the job, we see his scripts for broadcasting getting to grips more and more with his real interests and feelings.

In addition to both having demanding jobs, Eric and Eileen Blair moved house three times during the war owing to bomb damage: from Baker Street to 111 Langford Court in St John's Wood in 1941; from there, in the summer of 1942, to 10a Mortimer Crescent in Kilburn; and in October 1944, after three or four months at a friend's flat near Baker Street, to 27b Canonbury

Square, Islington.[10] House moving, added to Home Guard duty at night, a full-time job during the week, at least one intermittent love affair while remaining mainly faithful to his wife, and gardening at the cottage in Wallington at weekends, kept Orwell fully occupied. His mother, Ida Blair, and his sister Avril, had moved from Southwold to London in 1941 and were living in a small flat in Hampstead.[11] Both of them were working to support the war effort, his mother as an assistant at Selfridges, Avril in a factory.

Ida was in poor health and died of heart failure precipitated by bronchitis at New End Hospital in Hampstead on 19 March 1943 with Orwell at her bedside. He had also been with his father when he died of cancer in Southwold in 1939. 'All very painful and upsetting but I was glad when the poor old man went because he was 82 & had suffered a lot his last few months.'[12] All countries combined, the war killed over 20 million military personnel and from 30 to 55 million civilians.[13] In England 60,000 civilians were killed by German bombing

---

[10] Chronology in *Letters*, 497-98.

[11] Bowker, p. 282.

[12] Letter to Gorer, loc. cit.

[13] Alan Axelrod, *The Real History of World War II – A New Look at the Past*. New York: Sterling, 2008, pp 354-5.

raids,[14] and Eileen's much loved brother, an army doctor, was killed at Dunkirk in 1940. Death, loss and fear were thus a pervasive part of the atmosphere. Although Orwell did not write much about how all this affected him personally, it helps to explain some of the heightened awareness that went into what he did write.

'A writer's work is not something he takes out of his brain like tins of soup out of a storeroom. He has to create it day by day out of his contact with people and things,' he wrote in an article about Henry Miller towards the end of 1942.[15] His own work during that year shows him doing just that, in perhaps the busiest and most intensely social period of his life. During the spring of 1942 he reopened his diary to keep track of some of the thoughts that might not do for immediate public attention. It shows him trying to keep focused on his real concerns, and provides an outlet for his pessimism as things get worse in the summer. In the autumn the diary petered out, however, as more and more of his attention went into the BBC work. As the end of the year approaches and the

---

[14] Andrew Marr, *The Making of Modern Britain.* London: Macmillan, 2009; p. 354.

[15] 'The End of Henry Miller.' *Complete Works, vol. XIV, Keeping Our Little Corner Clean*, p. 219.

war news improves, a new note of confidence begins to dominate his writings. All of this contributed significantly to what we now know as Orwell's way of seeing things.[16]

---

[16] Christopher Hitchens defined the term 'Orwellian' as 'crushing tyranny and fear and conformism' when said of a state of affairs, and 'unquenchable resistance to these terrors' when said of a piece of writing. In *Why Orwell Matters*. New York: Basic Books, 2002; p. 5.

# Becoming Propaganda-Minded

## Winter and Spring 1942

### Fighting defeatism

In his 'London Letter' to American readers dated 1 January 1942, Orwell mentions that Dylan Thomas is doing jobs for the BBC and the Ministry of Information. 'So is nearly everybody that used to be a writer, and most of us rapidly going native.'[17] It implies that one cannot write for the government and still be a proper writer, but the tenor of this whole piece suggests the opposite. Not only is he writing strongly but he extends his propaganda work into this unofficial, spare-time article by launching an attack on pacifism. He has already 'gone native', but, as he himself could

---

[17] 'London Letter' dated 1 January 1942, in March–April 1942 issue of *Partisan Review*. *Works XIII*, p. 113.

perhaps agree as an anti-colonialist, that is not always or necessarily a bad thing. Winston Churchill had got into broadcasting as well, and it was not doing his writing ability any obvious harm.

'Since we probably have ahead of us a long and exhausting war in which morale will be all-important', Orwell says at the beginning of his letter, he proposes to survey some of the currents of thought affecting it. They consist mainly of confusions helped along by enemy propaganda and surreptitiously fascist sympathies among the English. Of particular interest to him here are the pacifists he describes in a section on 'leftwing defeatism'. As a left-wing novelist whose protagonists always ended up defeated, it was important for Orwell's own moral clarity, as well as that of his readers, to get this right.

With the out-and-out, turn-the-other-cheek pacifists you come upon the much stranger phenomenon of people who have started by renouncing violence ending by championing Hitler. The antisemitic motif is very strong though usually soft-pedalled in print. But not many English pacifists have the intellectual courage to think their thoughts down to the roots, and since there is no answer to the charge that pacifism is objectively pro-Fascist, nearly all pacifist literature is forensic – i.e. specializes in avoiding awkward questions.[18]

It sounds like a typical Orwell overstatement to say that pacifism is *objectively* pro-fascist, and there is *no* answer to that charge, but it is more like a simplification: however pacifists may feel about it, their position is more of a help than a hindrance to fascism.

He had worked this out a few months earlier in a review of a pacifist novel, *No Such Liberty*. The choice, he had said there, was not between good and evil but between two evils: 'You can let the Nazis rule the world; that is evil; or you can overthrow them by war, which is also evil.'[19] Everyone had to make that choice in the current situation, he argued, and 'the notion that you can somehow defeat violence by submitting to it is simply a flight from fact.'[20] He had written that for *The Adelphi*, whose pacifist editor (John Middleton Murry) praised it for being cogent but

---

[18] Ibid., p. 110.

[19] 'No, Not One'. Review of *No Such Liberty* by Alex Comfort, *The Adelphi*, October 1941. *Works XIII*, p. 43.

[20] Ibid.

disagreed because he held it 'as a matter of religious faith' that 'we should "resist not evil"', and that Hitlerism was 'the scourge of the Lord.'[21] The rejoinder makes Orwell look more cogent still. The 'London Letter' with his renewed attack on pacifism came out in the March issue of *Partisan Review*, detonating a volley of ripostes. These and his response to them, which he wrote in the summer, were printed in the September issue. The argument displays not only a hardening of his personal conviction during his BBC time but increased power to argue for it publicly, as we shall see.

In the meantime he had to get on with his main work of maintaining the fighting spirit with radio talks. In the script for a talk on the meaning of sabotage, lasting ten minutes and ten seconds (worth noting for the kind of precision now required), he covers the whole distance from the origin of the word to the practical power it represents. 'Once, many years ago, some working men who had a grievance against their employer threw their sabots into a piece of machinery while it was running, and thus damaged it. This action

---

[21] Ibid., pp. 43-44.

was nicknamed sabotage...'[22] It had to be written that simply so it could be read out intelligibly by Balraj Sahni and get through to listeners whose first language was not English. The effect was a fairy-story style which was new for Orwell but thoroughly well practised by the time he got back to his 'real writing' in 1943.

Sabotage, this piece explained, was the last resort of a conquered population against their own enslavement, but it was invincible. What the fascists wanted from their conquests was not more living-space or 'Asia for the Asiatics', but more slaves for the self-appointed master races.

> The German picture of Europe is of two hundred million people all working from morning to night and turning over the products of their work to Germany, and getting in return just as much help as will keep them from dying of starvation. The Japanese picture of Asia is similar. To some extent the German aims have already been achieved. But it is just here that the importance of sabotage comes in.

---

[22] 'The Meaning of Sabotage', in the series 'Through Eastern Eyes', broadcast on 29 January 1942. *Works XIII*, p. 142.

The Germans were reporting more and more executions for sabotage to discourage people from doing it, but in a way, Orwell suggested, the trend was encouraging: it showed that there were more and more 'brave men who have grasped the nature of German rule and are willing to risk their lives to overthrow it.' They reflected 'the immense power and importance of the ordinary working man,' who always had it in his power to throw the oppressor's systems out of gear.

A few blows from a sledge hammer, in the right place, can stop a power station working. One tug at the wrong signal lever can wreck a train. Quite a small charge of explosive can sink a ship. One box of matches, or one match, can destroy hundreds of tons of cattle fodder. Now, there is no doubt that acts of this kind are being carried out all over Europe and in greater and *greater* numbers.

Because of this, everyone had to be watched by 'huge armies of police, SS-men, ordinary uniformed police, plain-clothed police and spies and provocateurs of all kinds.' This reduced the manpower available for further conquests.

Not everyone was heroic enough for that kind of war work, but that was where passive sabotage came in, offering splendid opportunities for slackers, cowards and standard Orwellian antiheroes, who could be just as useful and were harder to catch. 'When Hitler finally falls,' this thought for the day concludes, 'the European workers who idled, shammed sickness, wasted material and damaged machinery in the factories, will have played an important part in his destruction.' Here strategic thinking, personal interest and workaday propaganda go well together.

## Finding a tenable position

Gandhi, with his non-violent resistance movement in India, could wholeheartedly agree, and that was the problem: sabotage could be used as effectively against the British as against the Japanese who at that point were rapidly supplanting them on the eastern side of the empire. To discourage its use against the Allies while encouraging it against the Axis, Orwell needed to show the difference between the two evils of old-fashioned British imperialism and the modern 'gangster fascist' variety. T. S. Eliot had brought out *A Choice of Kipling's Verse* in December 1941, and these popular jingles by such a wholehearted believer in the empire provided a good opportunity to examine the old British version. It was a culture into which Orwell had been born, in Bengal in 1903. He was taken to England with his mother and sister the following year, but his father continued to work in the Opium Department of the Indian Civil Service until his retirement in 1912. Orwell followed in his footsteps, serving as an increasingly disaffected imperial policeman in Burma for five years after leaving Eton. This background of involvement in the Empire had helped to make him eligible for his current job and was now something about which he needed to be as clear as possible, if only to fulfil his contractual obligation. When Kipling died, in 1935, Orwell had written in *New English Weekly*, 'I worshipped Kipling at thirteen, loathed him at seventeen, enjoyed him at twenty, despised him at twenty-five, and now again rather admire him.'[23] The luxury of that kind of floating with whatever current of feeling happened to carry him along had gone with other peacetime pleasures.

His essay on Kipling for *Horizon* in February 1942 was thus responding to a chronic ambivalence as well as an acute pressure. He

---

[23] *Essays 2*, p. 183.

needed to decide, so he did: 'Kipling *is* a jingo imperialist,' he asserts, differing with Eliot who had tried to defend him. 'He *is* morally insensitive and aesthetically disgusting. It is better to start by admitting that and then to try and find out why it is that he survives while the refined people who have sniggered at him seem to wear so badly.'[24] Instead of dismissing him, he deplores *both* the 'bouncing, vulgar vitality' with which Kipling had expressed the self-confidence of the British, *and* the facility with which people without responsibility could, in Kipling's adroit phrase, 'make mock of uniforms that guard you while you sleep'. The enduring popular appeal of Kipling, as Orwell saw it now, came as much from the obviousness of his ideas as from the deftness with which he expressed them. This he thought was an effect on the writer's intelligence of responsibility.

One reason for Kipling's power as a good bad[25] poet I have already suggested – his sense of

---

[24] 'Rudyard Kipling', *Horizon*, February 1942. *Works XIII*, p. 150.

[25] Christopher Hitchens referred to 'the good-bad book, as G. K. Chesterton (later plagiarized by Orwell) was to term this tempting genre' in *Hitch-22* (London: Atlantic, 2011, p. 57).

responsibility, which made it possible for him to have a world-view, even though it happened to be a false one. Although he had no connection with any political party, Kipling was a Conservative, a thing that does not exist nowadays. Those who now call themselves Conservatives are either Liberals, Fascists or the accomplices of Fascists. He identified himself with the ruling power and not with the opposition. In a gifted writer this seems to us strange and even disgusting, but it did have the advantage of giving Kipling a certain grip on reality. The ruling power is always faced with the question, "In such and such circumstances, what would you *do*?", whereas the opposition is not obliged to take responsibility or make any real decisions.[26]

As a salaried bureaucrat and a patriot, Orwell was now a supporter of the ruling power himself, and so could base the assertion on his own experience. However 'strange and disgusting' his own position may have seemed to him, he had chosen it, and the sense of responsibility that came with it was giving him a fuller world-view and a firmer grip on reality than he had had before.

---

[26] *Works XIII*, p. 160.

But Kipling had 'sold out to the British governing class,' and that had 'warped his political judgment.' Whether or not his diagnosis was correct, Orwell was improving his chances of avoiding that pitfall himself by naming it. He has the appearance here of measuring himself against his predecessor, while approaching a success that was in some ways similar. Both writers became by-words for their kind of deeply English and politically loaded literature. And, Orwell noted, 'Kipling is the only English writer of our time who has added phrases to the language.' He cites 'East is East and West is West' and 'the white man's burden' as examples, as well as others that have since faded out. He of course was to achieve that distinction with his own coinages such as 'some are more equal than others', 'Big Brother is watching you', 'newspeak', 'doublethink', 'thoughtcrime' etc. which are such common currency now that they have themselves become components of a kind of 'duckspeak'.[27] Like Kipling too, Orwell arguably found his way into his full strength as a writer via working as a committed and sincere supporter of the

[27] 'Not speech in the true sense: it was a noise uttered in unconsciousness, like the quacking of a duck.' *Nineteen Eighty-Four*. Harmondsworth: Penguin, 1954, p. 47.

establishment. It was certainly worth the trouble to revisit the work of this highly influential writer to assess both the bad and the good effects of that commitment.

Meanwhile, the object of Kipling's devotion was dissolving as the sun continued to set on the British Empire. A massive setback occurred on 15 February 1942 with the fall of Singapore, in which 70,000 Allied soldiers were taken prisoner by the Japanese. Churchill, with his knack of making bad news a means of deepening determination, called it 'the worst disaster and largest capitulation in British history,'[28] but Orwell as a mere talks producer in the Empire Service did not have that kind of latitude. His job was to comment in a positive way and he did his best. In his news review of 14 February, while the defeat was still in progress, he presented what he called 'a realistic and un-varnished view of the situation.' Contemplating the prospect of Japan gaining control of the Indian Ocean and Germany breaking through to the Persian Gulf, he concluded that 'even if this grandiose plan should succeed in its entirety, it would not give the Axis

---

[28] Winston Churchill, *The Hinge of Fate* (1951). London: Penguin, 2005; p. 81.

Powers victory, unless the Allied peoples of America, Soviet Russia, Britain and China lost heart. It still remains true that the balance of power, both in men, materials and industrial plant, is heavily against the Axis Powers.'[29]

Losing heart is easier to guard against if you have the upper hand physically, and for Indians it was not so clear which was more disheartening: continued domination by the British or a new Japanese variety. This made the task of maintaining pro-British sentiments both more urgent and more difficult. Orwell called for 'resolution, calmness and faith in final victory' and asserted that 'if the great peoples of China and India stand together, they cannot be overwhelmed even by the most powerful and ruthless aggressor.' It was probably true, and the phrases were perhaps unavoidable, but they must have sounded the same as all the other competitive quacking on the airwaves at that time.

Churchill of course still believed in the Empire and was especially fond of Kipling's 'If',[30] but could see that new sources of hope were needed

---

[29] *Works XIII*, p. 179.

[30] 'If you can meet with Triumph and Disaster / And treat those two imposters just the same;' for instance; Churchill, p. 386.

in India. He sent Sir Stafford Cripps, who was now Lord Privy Seal and a member of the War Cabinet, to rally support in India for Britain in return for self-government after the war. Nicknamed 'the red squire', and classed as a 'high-minded toff',[31] as Orwell himself sometimes was, Cripps had achieved fame as a barrister defending working-class causes. His socialism, unlike Orwell's, came from inherited family values rather than rebellion: his father, Lord Parmoor, was a prominent Labour MP, and one of his aunts, Beatrice Webb, was a founder of Britain's Labour Party. Stafford was viewed at that time as a potential alternative to Churchill, whose abilities and beliefs were in doubt while the war was going badly. Russia's alliance with Britain was widely attributed to Cripps, as he had, at his own initiative, been Ambassador to Moscow from 1940 to early 1942.

Perhaps in the hope of finding someone to believe in for himself, as well as for the Indians, Orwell talked Cripps up as much as possible in his news reviews. 'He is a man of great personal austerity, a vegetarian, a teetotaller and a devout

---

[31] Peter Clarke, *The Cripps Version*. London: Penguin, 2002, p. 107.

practising Christian,'[32] he told them in the build-up before Cripps's visit. That should have made a good impression on Gandhi's followers, but he himself disliked all those virtues with the possible exception of austerity. He gave that one an extra fillip with a touching hagiographical detail: 'So simple are his manners that he is to be seen every morning having breakfast in a cheap London eating house, among working men and office employees.'

## Entering a new phase

If the job had been confined to this kind of bland and rather silly-sounding diplomacy, his talents might indeed have atrophied, but there were opportunities for exercising some of them more vigorously during work time. Earlier in the week he had broadcast a half-hour talk on 'Literature between the Wars' for which he had marshalled extensive knowledge while indulging his quirky tendency to overstate his case. He called his talk 'The Re-discovery of Europe' to characterize the difference between English literature before and after the First World War. Before it there was 'a

---

[32] Weekly News Review 14, 14 March 1942. *Works XIII*, p. 225.

complete unawareness of anything outside the contemporary English scene'[33] in writers such as Shaw, Wells, Kipling, Bennett, Hardy, Housman and Rupert Brooke. After it, writers such as Joyce, Eliot, Pound, Huxley, D. H. Lawrence and Wyndham Lewis 'broke the cultural circle in which England had existed for something like a century. They re-established contact with Europe, and they brought back the sense of history and the possibility of tragedy.' There is a sense of Orwell's own liberation in this perspective as he ends bracingly: 'On that basis all subsequent English literature that matters twopence has rested, and the development that Eliot and the others started, back in the closing years of the last war, has not yet run its course.' In retrospect it sounds like a personal resolve to write something that matters twopence himself.

While drawing the contrast between the defunct and the new kind of writing, he had dismissed the 'Science-worship' of H. G. Wells along with the 'shallow Fabian progressivism' of Bernard Shaw. Both these revered figures were still alive, aged 76 and 86 respectively, and

---

[33] 'The Re-discovery of Europe' in *The Listener*, 19 March 1942. *Works XIII*, p. 211.

kicking. Shaw let it pass but Wells sent an acid response to *The Listener*, in which Orwell's talk had been published. He also wrote an angry personal letter to Orwell it, telling him to 'read my early works you shit.'[34] In his younger days Orwell had been an admirer of Wells, especially for his science fiction. Such peevishness must have added to his disenchantment with him now. Other indignant letters appeared in *The Listener* as well.

In this area of cultural studies, working for the BBC was comparable to getting a university education, only better: free from the competitively orthodox or money-making thinking bred by academia but still having to perform to a high standard under plenty of well-qualified scrutiny. Usually it is Orwell's time of penury in Paris in his mid-twenties that is seen as his equivalent of a university education, but the BBC period probably drove him to study both harder and more productively.

To hold fast to his own point of view, he reopened his wartime diary on 14 March 1942, 'after an interval of about 6 months, the war being

---

[34] D. J. Taylor, p. 305.

once again in a new phase.'[35] He does not define that phase but since his last entry, on 28 August 1941, a lot had happened. The Germans had failed to capture Leningrad and Moscow, the US had entered the war (on 8 December 1941, directly after Japan's attack on Pearl Harbour); Singapore had fallen; the Germans were in deadlock with the British in North Africa but seemed likely to prevail there; and there were now 26 countries in the 'United Nations' against Germany, Japan and Italy. Now that it is history, it seems obvious that the Axis powers would be defeated, but Japan was still making alarming progress in the Western Pacific, the Russians were thought to be liable to cave in or make a new pact with Germany, a German invasion of Britain was still thought likely, Churchill, then aged 68, looked too incompetent to do much good, and America's war aims were not necessarily the same as those of Britain.

'I have now been in the BBC about six months,' he continued. 'Shall remain in it if the political changes I foresee come off, otherwise probably not. Its atmosphere is something

---

[35] Peter Davison, ed., *George Orwell Diaries*. London: Harvill Secker, 2009; p. 321.

halfway between a girls' school and a lunatic asylum...' He must have taken some therapeutic pleasure in writing this, like Winston Smith voluptuously penning 'DOWN WITH BIG BROTHER' in his diary. The political changes he was hoping for included a fair deal for Indian independence and a shift towards a classless society in Britain, both of which Cripps also seemed to favour. If Orwell's efforts could help bring those about, his note to himself implies, they would be worth making, even in an environment he found so pathological and childish. However, he was not ideally placed to help, and did not have enough access to the information he needed. For instance he notes, 'The actual date of Cripps's departure for India has not been given out, but presumably he has gone by this time,' though in fact Cripps did not leave until eight days later.[36]

The diary goes on '...all we are doing at present is useless or slightly worse than useless. Our radio strategy is even more hopeless than our military strategy. Nevertheless one rapidly becomes propaganda-minded and develops a cunning one did not previously have.' To illustrate this, he describes how he has been alleging in his

---

[36] Ibid., 321, and note 1, p. 323.

35

News Reviews that the Japanese are preparing to attack Russia, not because he thinks they are but because there are some advantages to be gained from raising that expectation, or from being thought to think so. 'All propaganda is lies,' he tells himself, 'even when one is telling the truth. I don't think this matters so long as one knows what one is doing, and why.' Even before he went to Spain he had been stressing the need for 'intelligent propaganda'[37] as a way to fight fascism, but his present combination of professionalism and detachment is new. Knowing what one was doing meant not selling out like Kipling or, as he put it later, like G. K. Chesterton, 'a writer of considerable talent who chose to suppress both his sensibilities and his intellectual honesty in the cause of Roman Catholic propaganda.'[38]

The diary was a means of avoiding that fate by recording real perceptions and feelings, however simple, rather than suppressing them. Other examples from that spring of 1942: 'Crocuses

---

[37] *The Road to Wigan Pier* (1937). Harmondsworth: Penguin, 1961; p. 202.

[38] 'Notes on Nationalism' (1945), in *Decline of the English Murder and Other Essays*. Harmondsworth: Penguin, 1965; p. 160.

now full out. One seems to catch glimpses of them dimly through a haze of war news' (27 March). 'Greatly depressed by the apparent failure of the Cripps mission' (1 April). 'We are all drowning in filth. When I talk to anyone or read the writings of anyone who has any axe to grind, I feel that intellectual honesty and balanced judgement have simply disappeared from the face of the earth' (27 April).

# A Firmer Grip on Reality

## Summer 1942

### The real man?

In May Orwell's thoughts returned to Dickens, a
fellow 'writer-with-a-purpose' using the mass
medium of his day to entertain and edify the
public. Dickens wrote above all to be listened to,
and it was that kind of power that Orwell was
learning about through direct experimentation
now. Reviewing for *The Observer* a recent study
by Edmund Wilson,[39] he pondered over the
contrast between the 'certain native goodness'
which permeates Dickens's novels, and the
assertion of Katey Perugini, his last surviving

---

[39] Edmund Wilson, 'Dickens: the Two Scrooges', in *The
Wound and the Bow.* New York: Oxford University
Press, 1941; republished by Ohio University Press, 1997,
pp 3-85.

daughter, that he was '"a wicked man – a very wicked man." It is a strange epitaph for the author of "The Pickwick Papers".'[40]

Wilson had built on Gladys Storey's *Dickens and Daughter* (London: Frederick Muller, 1939) as evidence for what Orwell now saw as 'a definitely criminal strain' in Dickens. Orwell's own essay on him in 1939 had made him a hero with a special set of mainly harmless compulsions and disabilities. Dickens came across there as the fearless upholder of human decency and freedom of thought – exactly the qualities threatened by fascism. At that time Orwell had been dismissive about the author's mistreatment of his wife: 'it no more invalidates his work than the second best bed invalidates *Hamlet*,' he said.[41] That was nicely put, but now he was confronted by something more awkward. 'What is remarkable is not that Dickens should have indulged in a mistress but that he evidently behaved with

---

[40] Review of *The Wound and the Bow* by Edmund Wilson, *The Observer*, 10 May 1942. *Works XIII*, 315.

[41] George Orwell, 'Charles Dickens'. In *Decline of the English Murder and Other Essays*. Harmondsworth: Penguin, 1965; p. 81.

abominable cruelty towards his wife, and at least very tyrannically towards his children.'[42]

Judging by his own extramarital affairs, at least one of which was in progress at the time,[43] Orwell was not against 'indulging', but cruelty and tyranny were another matter. Unable to condone them or to reject Dickens, he called the contrast between his 'literary emanation' and his private life 'baffling', and left it as a variant of the Jekyll and Hyde enigma. 'One is forced to believe in a sort of split personality, in which David Copperfield rather than Charles Dickens is the real man,' he concluded interestingly. Why not the other way round?

Some such split can be seen between George Orwell the adroitly honest and kind-hearted author and Eric Blair the awkward, perhaps sadistic and anyway blundering egoist or 'complete pain'[44] suggested by some of those who

---

[42] *Works XIII*, p. 314-5

[43] With Inez Holden. See Crick, pp. 423-424, for example, and Bowker, p. 284. Other involvements include Hetta Crouse (later Empson), Stevie Smith, and 'a secretary'.

[44] Expression used in an email from D. J. Taylor to correct my pro-Orwell bias in his dealings with Victor Gollancz.

knew him and his biographers.[45] The name 'Orwell' came into existence, like 'Copperfield', with its similar connotations of valuable metal, as the fictitious narrator of an imaginative memoir (*Down and Out in Paris and London*). It was a pen-name he chose at random to conceal the author's identity, so as not to upset his parents or jeopardize his teaching job. Now, if it was necessary to choose between the invented character and the flesh-and-blood person, not everyone would agree that the real McCoy must be the intangible but more likeable one. Dostoevsky was troubled by the same kind of anomaly in himself, and is said to have taken the opportunity to ask Dickens about it when he visited him in London in 1862. This is how he is said to have recorded their discussion:

The person he [the writer] sees most of, most often, actually every day, is himself. When it comes to a question of why a man does something else, it's the author's own actions which make him understand, or fail to understand, the sources of human action.

---

[45] See also 'The case against' in Taylor, 350-52, and the disparaging memories of his flat-mates Rayner Heppenstall and Michael Sayers (Bowker, 176-7).

Dickens told me the same thing when I met him at the office of his magazine … his attacks of helpless enmity towards those who were helpless and looked to him for comfort, his shrinking from those whom he ought to love, being used up in what he wrote. There were two people in him, he told me: one who feels as he ought to feel and one who feels the opposite. From the one who feels the opposite I make my evil characters, from the one who feels as a man ought to feel I try to live my life. Only two people? I asked.[46]

Whether this exchange took place or was itself fictitious, it is revealing about the relation between the novelist's characters and himself.

Orwell, in a later essay, on Salvador Dali, was able to put the difficulty more succinctly than before, partly because his judgement went the other way: 'One ought to be able to hold in one's head simultaneously the two facts that Dali is a good draughtsman and a disgusting human being. The one does not invalidate the other or, in a sense, affect the other.'[47] But a draughtsman is not

---

[46] Quoted by Claire Tomalin in *Charles Dickens – A Life*. London: Viking, 2011, p. 322.

[47] 'Benefit of Clergy' (1944), in *Decline*.

necessarily an artist, and in the case of a word-artist the idea of a disgusting character producing admirable work can be especially difficult to hold in one's head. It was hard for Orwell in the case of Kipling 'with his jingoism and brutality,' for instance, so he settled for the notion of a 'good bad poet' but with emphasis on the 'bad'. For Dickens he retains the emphasis on 'good', but his regard has had to be a bit more beady-eyed.

The present situation called for someone who was not only worthy of respect but alive, and in a position to do something. For a little while Stafford Cripps seemed eligible for that role, and Orwell went to see him the following week. 'I saw Cripps on Wednesday, the first time I had actually spoken to him. Rather well impressed. He was more approachable and easy-going than I expected, and quite ready to answer questions. Though aged 53 some of his movements are almost boyish. On the other hand he has a decidedly red nose.'[48]

Orwell's interest in him was work-related as much as personal. During the same week in mid-May he was lining up speakers for his latest idea for putting the present situation in perspective: a

_____

[48] Entry on 15 May 1942, *Diaries*, p. 338.

series of talks on the future of India, entitled 'A.D. 2000' – not bad for 1942. He chose the following subjects: '400 Millions: the Indian Population Problem', 'Future of Indian Agriculture', 'India in the Steel Age', 'Future of Education in India'. 'Industrialisation in India', and 'East or West: India's Cultural Future'.[49] Thinking about the future to get out of the clutches of immediate worries was perhaps the greatest idea he had taken from H. G. Wells and one that he would take up again after the war, with stunning effect. With access to whoever might know best about such matters (then as now, most people welcomed the chance to air their expertise), he could make use of their brains and perhaps measure his own against them while he was at it.

In addition, people in high positions generate a kind of social electricity which is interesting in itself. Cripps as a political celebrity had that aura for the moment, and Orwell took the trouble to note its effect on him:

As I waited trying to talk to his secretary, a phrase I always remember on these occasions came into my mind – "shivering in ante-rooms".

---

[49] *Works XIII*, p. 534.

In eighteenth-century biographies you always read about people waiting on their patrons and "shivering in anterooms". It is one of those ready-made phrases like "leave no stone unturned", and yet how true it is as soon as you get anywhere near politics, or even the more expensive kind of journalism.[50]

For all his distrust of the powers that be, he had the usual physiological response to a representative of them, like that of the other animals to the top pigs in *Animal Farm*.[51] Not all Labour leaders had the same effect on him though, or if they did he chose to react against it in his diary: a few days later he noted, 'Attlee reminds me of nothing so much as a recently dead fish, before it has had time to stiffen.'[52]

Cripps's image as a good alternative to Churchill was short-lived, as he possessed neither the conviction to mount a challenge nor the opportunity to effect any significant change of policy. Any potential he may have had as a

---

[50] Entry for 15 May 1942, *Diaries*, p. 338-9.

[51] E.g., 'It was noticed that they wagged their tails to him, as the other dogs had been used to do to Mr. Jones. *Animal Farm*, London: Penguin, 1989, p. 36.

[52] Entry for 19 May 1942, Diaries, p. 339.

kindred spirit for Orwell also quickly faded. Two weeks after first meeting him, he spent an evening chatting with Cripps and 'some literary people' (William Empson, Jack Common, David Owen, Norman Cameron and Guy Burgess)[53] and soon found himself baffled again, and disappointed.

Cripps said several things that amazed and slightly horrified me. One was that many people whose opinion was worth considering believed that the war would be over by October – i.e. that Germany would be flat out by that time. When I said that I should look on that as a disaster pure and simple (because if the war were won as easily as that there would have been no real upheaval here and the American millionaires would still be in situ) he appeared not to understand.

One can sympathize with Cripps for not understanding. The view of the war as primarily an opportunity to redistribute wealth was not universally held, although it was common: J. B. Priestly argued for it in *Picture Post* that June, calling the war 'our great chance to fashion a

---

[53] Entry for 7 June 1942, *Diaries*, pp. 343-4.

really healthy society.'[54] Orwell found Cripps's incomprehension symptomatic of 'the official mind, which sees everything as a problem in administration' and does not realize that 'most of those who have power don't care a damn about the world as a whole and are only intent on feathering their own nests.'[55]

In addition to seeing that as the generic problem, Orwell suspected there was a personal one as well:

I can't help feeling a strong impression that Cripps has already been got at. Not with money or anything of that kind of course, nor even by flattery and the sense of power, which in all probability he genuinely doesn't care about: but simply by responsibility, which automatically makes a man timid. Besides, as soon as you are in power your perspectives are foreshortened. Perhaps a bird's eye view is as distorted as a worm's eye view.

In reality Cripps was probably looking got at because he was being prevented from doing much.

---

[54] J. B. Priestley, 'Britain's Silent Revolution'. *Picture Post*, 27 June 1942.

[55] Entry for 7 June 1942, *Diaries*, p. 344.

But the idea that responsibility makes a man timid is striking, and may have been suggested to Orwell by his own experience of it in his war job. He could have taken its perceived effects on Cripps as a warning.

## Real events

First-hand experience was making it clearer than ever to Orwell that the workings of political institutions, including the BBC, could not offer him much hope. Unlike Churchill, he was unaffected by the sense of significance parliamentary procedures could offer, and had experienced them as 'dreary rubbish' when he went to the House of Commons to listen to the debate on India. 'This is the twilight of parliamentary democracy,' he told his diary on that occasion, 'and these people are simply ghosts gibbering in some corner while the real events happen elsewhere.'[56]

He wrote about one such event in his diary on 11 June, just four days later:

The Germans announce over the wireless that as the inhabitants of a Czech village called Ladice

---

[56] Entry for 29 April 1942, *Diaries*, p. 336.

[sic for Lidice] (about 1200 inhabitants) were guilty of harbouring the assassins of Heydrich they have shot all the males in the village, sent all the women to concentration camps, sent all the children to be 're-educated', razed the whole village to the ground and changed its name.[57]

In the diary the event led to a reflection on how atrocities are 'believed in or disbelieved in according to political predilection, with utter non-interest in the facts and with complete willingness to alter one's beliefs as soon as the political scene alters.'[58] On the radio two days later he referred to the same event in some of the same words, introducing it as 'a comparatively small item of news, which is nevertheless worth reporting because it shows more clearly than whole books could do, what Fascism means.' What makes it usable is the fact that it cannot be dismissed as an Allied propaganda invention to vilify the Germans

---

[57] Entry for 11 June, ibid., p. 345. Reinhard Heydrich had chaired the Wannsee conference which on 20 January 1942 adopted the 'final solution' policy and been the leading proponent of its implementation. The association of his assassins with the village of Lidice turned out to be false.

[58] Ibid., 356.

since they themselves had broadcast it. Orwell makes this point vehemently:

> But more significant than the act, is the impudence with which it is broadcast to the world, almost as though it was something to be proud of. And most significant of all is the fact that more than three years after their seizure of Czechoslovakia, the Germans are compelled to commit these barbarities in order to hold down a people whom they pretend to be benefitting by their wise and disinterested rule.[59]

At this point he gives the impression of being able to think his thoughts through to a sense of truth more vigorously for broadcasting than in his diary or elsewhere. His sense of the significance of the event was also accurate. Heydrich was perhaps the strongest and most able of Hitler's supporters, and the Germans were unwittingly displaying their sense of having suffered a serious setback.

Other real events that summer included the agreement on 20 June between Churchill and Roosevelt to pool American and British resources

---

[59] Weekly News Review 26, 13 June 1942; *Works XIII*, p. 360.

for building an atomic bomb in America,[60] the fall of Tobruk in Libya on 21 June with 33,000 Allied prisoners taken, a failed assassination attempt by a 'crackpate' on Churchill on his way home from America on 25 June,[61] and the compliance of the French authorities with the German 'final solution' policy by sending 30,000 Jews to concentration camps on one day alone (16 July).[62] All these events reflect power only to kill people, but the Oxford Committee for Famine Relief, now Oxfam, was founded at the end of July 1942, and William Beveridge was doing good work – in obscurity but to be revealed soon – with his interdepartmental inquiry into the coordination of the social services.

Churchill's growing record of failure on all three military fronts – North Africa, Europe and the Pacific – led to a vote of censure which was taken in the House of Commons on 2 July. Orwell summed up the outcome sourly: 'Vote of censure

---

[60] Winston Churchill, *The Hinge of Fate* (1951). London: Penguin, 2005, p. 341.

[61] 'Crackpates are a special danger to public men, as they do not have to worry about the "get away"'. *The Hinge of Fate*, p. 350.

[62] *The Hutchinson Chronology of World History*. Oxford: Helicon, 1998, p. 335.

defeated 475-25. The same trick as usual – the debate twisted into a demand for a vote of confidence in Churchill himself, which has to be given, since there is no one to take Churchill's place. ... I don't know how much longer this comedy can go on, but not much longer.'[63] He was right in a way: the situation would change in the autumn.

At that point in his experience the BBC seemed like little more than a part of the same comedy. On the day of the military disaster in Tobruk, he wrote in his diary not about that but his sense that they were 'putting sheer rubbish on the air.'

The thing that strikes one at the BBC – and it is evidently the same in various of the other departments – is not so much the moral squalor and the ultimate futility of what we are doing, as the feeling of frustration, the impossibility of getting anything done, even any successful piece of scoundrelism. Our policy is so ill-defined, the disorganization is so great, there are so many changes of plan and the fear and hatred of

---

[63] Entry for 3 July, *Diaries*, pp. 350-351.

intelligence are so all-pervading, that one cannot plan any kind of wireless campaign whatever.[64]

'Everyone very defeatist after the Libya business,'[65] he noted a few days later, and, as the diary shows, it affected his own morale too, however doggedly anti-defeatist he made his public comments. Any hope he may have had of helping to change the world by means of the BBC seems pretty well snuffed out – at least for the moment – and at the end of June he took a two-week fishing holiday. He stayed on a farm in the suggestively named village of Callow End in Worcestershire,[66] which was to furnish some of the names and details for *Animal Farm*.[67]

## The power of English words

The break gave him time to review Mulk Raj Anand's novel set in India, *The Sword and the Sickle*. Appearing in the July issue of *Horizon*, the review focuses on the English language itself, and its power as 'one weapon which our enemies

---

[64] 21 June, ibid., p. 348.

[65] 26 June, ibid., p. 350.

[66] Ibid. (n. 60)

[67] Bowker, p. 294.

cannot use against us.' Insofar as the outcome of the war depended on the influence wielded by language, English speakers had a definite advantage. 'Several other languages are spoken by larger numbers of people, but there is no other that has any claim to be a world-wide *lingua franca*.'[68] As an Indian, Anand had legitimate grievances against the British, but used their language to express them and to promote the alternative to imperialism, which was international socialism, Orwell reasoned. 'That is why at the beginning of this review I described the English language as a weapon of war. It is a funnel for ideas deadly to the Fascist view of life.'[69] He could equally well have said that on the air, and it reflects a conviction which was as personal as it was public.

By that time *Partisan Review* had sent Orwell some responses by pacifists to his 'London Letter' of January, inviting him to respond to their self-defensive attacks on him. He did this with gusto, wielding the weapon of English with accuracy and force.

---

[68] Works XIII, p. 379.
[69] Ibid., p. 381.

If Mr Savage and others imagine that one can somehow "overcome" the German army by lying on one's back, let them go on imagining it, but let them also wonder occasionally whether this is not an illusion due to security, too much money and a simple ignorance of the way in which things actually happen. ... Despotic governments can stand "moral force" till the cows come home; what they fear is physical force.'[70]

Having been down and out, having spent five months on the Aragon front, having a fascist bullet hole in his neck, and anyway being older and more experienced than his opponents, Orwell implies, he could claim to know things they did not know. After pointing out that he was against imperialism 'because I know something about it from the inside', he defended his BBC work, which he was doing with English and Indian left-wing intellectuals not 'to "fox the Indian masses" [of which George Woodcock had accused him] but because they know what a Fascist victory would mean to the chances of India's independence.' As for his earlier contributions to

---

[70] 'Pacifism and the War: A Controversy.' *Partisan Review*, September-October 1942.

a pacifist paper, 'Of course I have written for the *Adelphi*. Why not? I once wrote an article for a vegetarian paper. Does that make me a vegetarian?'

Finally Alex Comfort's accusation that he was 'intellectual-hunting' provides the occasion for a stirring finale:

I have used a lot of ink and done myself a lot of harm by attacking the successive literary cliques which have infested this country, not because they were intellectuals but precisely because they were *not* what I mean by true intellectuals. The life of a clique is about five years and I have been writing long enough to see three of them come and two go – the Catholic gang, the Stalinist gang, and the present Pacifist or, as they are sometimes nicknamed, Fascifist gang. My case against all of them is that they write mentally dishonest propaganda and degrade literary criticism to mutual arse-licking... It is just because I do take the function of the intelligentsia seriously that I don't like the sneers, libels, parrot-phrases and financially profitable back-scratching which flourish in our English literary world, and perhaps in yours too.

His counter-attack was harsher than the provocation but it also has a sense of fresh air and enjoyment about it, like going outdoors for some vigorous exercise after being cooped up in the office for too long. At heart he sympathized with the pacifist ideal and had been anti-war himself until August 1939 when he realized 'two things, first that I should be simply relieved when the long-dreaded war started, secondly, that I was patriotic at heart, would not sabotage or act against my own side, would support the war, would fight in it if possible.'[71] Not long after their dispute he became friendly with both George Woodcock and Alex Comfort.

'I am now making entries in this diary much more seldom than I used to,' he wrote at the end of July, 'for the reason that I literally have not any spare time.'[72] In reality the diary has more entries in August than any other month of 1942, and does not stop altogether till 5 November. What felt like less time for it may actually have been less need, now that he was finding ways to get to grips with his main concerns on the air and in print. 'And yet I am doing nothing that is not futility and have less

---

[71] 'My Country Right or Left', *Essays 1*, 590-591.

[72] Entry on 23 July 1942, *Diaries*, p. 354.

and less to show for the time I waste ... just footling around doing imbecile things.'[73] It is true that he had only written one proper article so far that summer, unless one counts the *Partisan Review* riposte; but he was to make up for it with a long and thoughtful one at the end of August.

'Something to show' would have been a book in progress, but at least the lull provided an opportunity to think about what such a book could be. If literature was a funnel for ideas, what were some examples? In August he started commissioning speakers for a new series he called 'Books that Changed the World'. These he defined as books which 'can be said to have actually influenced events directly by their impact on the big public.'[74] The ones he chose were *The Descent of Man, Uncle Tom's Cabin, Gulliver's Travels, The Social Contract, War and Peace, Das Kapital,* and *Mein Kampf.*[75] Their effects are debatable of course, but all seven books have in common some sense of revelation, for better or for worse. Once their worldview was presented, it seemed obvious to large numbers of readers. It

---

[73] Ibid.

[74] Commissioning letter to K. S. Shelvankar, 6 August 1942. *Works XIII*, p. 451.

[75] *Works XIV*, p. 368.

was for this kind of impact that he was to aim with the next two books of his own.

He continued the series of talks in 1943, this time focusing on what he called 'Oriental books, particularly religious books.'[76] These were less controversial from the point of view of affecting history: *The Koran*, *The Bible*, *The Upanishads*, *The Analects of Confucius*, *The Bhagavad Gita* and *The New Testament*.[77] His own view of religious faith was that it was obsolete, but its influence on human behaviour was obvious, and he was fond of the Christian tradition.[78] Harold

---

[76] Letter to Sirdar Ikbal Ali Shah, *Works XV*, p. 21.

[77] *Works XV*, 373. Melvin Bragg of the BBC continued this approach with a book called *12 Books that Changed the World* (London: Hodder & Stoughton, 2006), without attributing the idea to Orwell. His twelve, reflecting the comparative complexity of his mind, were: Isaac Newton's *Principia Mathematica*, *Married Love* by Marie Stopes, the *Magna Carta*, *The Rule Book of Association Football*, *On the Origin of Species* by Darwin, *On the Abolition of the Slave Trade* by William Wilberforce, *A Vindication of the Rights of Woman* by Mary Wollstonecraft, *Experimental Researches in Electricity* by Michael Faraday, *Patent Specification for Arkwright's Spinning Machine* by Richard Arkwright, *The King James Bible*, *The Wealth of Nations* by Adam Smith, and *The First Folio* of Shakespeare.

[78] See, for example, Peter Davison's 'Orwell: Religious and Ethical Values', *The Orwell Essay*, Finlay Publisher,

Nicolson in *Why Britain is at War* had exclaimed: 'Why should our lovely Christian code of honour surrender to this pagan brutality?'[79] Orwell could not have put it like that but his appeals to 'decency' have the same historical and emotional background.

The BBC was in fact offering him new opportunities for creative thinking, and in August he launched a literary discussion series called 'Voice'. The first edition involved Herbert Read, William Empson, Inez Holden and Mulk Raj Anand, discussing work by themselves, Dylan Thomas, Henry Treece, and Wordsworth, with Orwell as the presenter. Introducing it as a new kind of literary journal, he made an intriguing case for thinking about literature at such a time.

I suppose every second that we sit here at least one human being will be dying a violent death. It may seem a little dilettante to be starting a magazine concerned primarily with poetry at a moment when, quite literally, the fate of the world is being decided by bombs and bullets.

---

March to May 2008. Accessed at www.finaly-publisher.com on 5 July 2011.

[79] Harold Nicolson, *Why Britain in at War*. London: Penguin, 1939 and 2010, p. 135.

However, our magazine – 'Voice' we are calling it – isn't quite an ordinary magazine. To begin with it doesn't use up any paper or the labour of any printers or booksellers. All it needs is a little electrical power and half a dozen voices. It doesn't have to be delivered at your door, and you don't have to pay for it. It can't be described as a wasteful form of entertainment. Moreover, there are some of us who feel that it is exactly at times like the present that literature ought not to be forgotten. As a matter of fact, this business of pumping words into the ether, its potentialities and the actual uses it is put to, has its solemn side. According to some authorities wireless waves, or some wireless waves, don't merely circle our planet, but travel on endlessly through space at the speed of light, in which case what we are saying this afternoon should be audible in the great nebula in Orion nearly a million years hence. If there are intelligent beings there, as there well may be, … it won't hurt them to pick up a few specimens of twentieth century verse along with the swing music and latest wad of lies from Berlin.[80]

---

[80] "Voice" for Tuesday 11 August 1942. *Works XIII*, p. 459.

The departure of literature from paper was already under way. It is as hard to say now as it was then whether this is increasing the power of language or reducing it. Orwell was aware that the hypothetical listeners in Orion would be receiving an unlimited amount of 'tripe'[81] for every limited worthwhile item, but could have argued that the rarity of a good piece of work increases its value. In that case his efforts (and, who knows, perhaps even mine) to produce one or two may yet prove not to have been in vain. Subsequently, T. S. Eliot and other luminaries joined the 'Voice' programme, and photographs of these gatherings suggest that if Orwell thought he was wasting his time then, he was at least enjoying it.

On Friday 7 August US troops in the Pacific captured Henderson Airfield on Guadalcanal, one of the Solomon Islands. It was the first significant defeat for the Japanese and came to be seen as the beginning of the turning-point in the war. It might have boosted morale but was followed the next day by the passing of the Quit India Resolution by the Bombay session of the All India Congress Committee. This led to a campaign of civil disobedience during which Gandhi, Nehru and

---

[81] 'Poetry and the Microphone', *Essays 2*, p. 380.

other popular leaders were locked up by the British authorities, with Churchill's hearty approval. 'Terrible feeling of depression among the Indians and everyone sympathetic to India... It is strange, but quite truly the way the British Government is now behaving upsets me more than a military defeat.'[82] Broadcasting pro-British material required an even greater effort of concentration on what he saw as the essentials.

Despite the feeling of having too little time for such things, Orwell wrote one of his most revealing longer pieces during this period, probably at the end of August. 'On Looking Back on the Spanish War', was written for Alex Comfort's journal *New Road*.[83] In addition to reflecting on the squalor of war which had punctured any illusions he may have had about it, he set out some of the fears he was to explore five years later in *Nineteen Eighty-Four* : of 'the very concept of objective truth fading out of the world'; of 'a nightmare world in which the leader or some ruling clique controls not only the future but the past'; and of the fact that 'civilizations founded on

---

[82] Entry for 10 August 1942, *Diaries*, p. 359.

[83] For the text and probable dates of writing and publication see *Works XIII*, pp. 497-511.

slavery have lasted for such periods as four thousand years' and could do so again. Perhaps because it was for a pacifist publication, he felt able to display his humane side here with an anecdote about a Fascist he could not bring himself to shoot. The target was running with one hand holding up his trousers. It meant he was a fellow human being after all.

The defining paradox of his life comes into full view here: on the one hand the horror and terror of war, and on the other the sense that there are some things worth suffering and fighting for. He returns to the image he used in *Homage to Catalonia* of the Italian militiaman who had come to represent for him what the war was about. 'When I remember – oh how vividly! – his shabby uniform and the fierce, pathetic, innocent face, the complex side-issues of the war seem to fade away and I see clearly that there was at any rate no doubt as to who was in the right.' It was rare for Orwell to write 'oh' and use the exclamation mark, and it was quite some time since he had seen himself as a potential poet,[84] but he ends the essay with a piece of verse. The last two of his nine stanzas are:

---

[84] See D. J. Taylor, 'Orwell's Poetry', *The Orwell Essay*, Finlay Publisher, December 2008 – January 2009. Accessed at www.finaly-publisher.com on 5 July 2011.

Your name and your deeds were forgotten
Before your bones were dry,
And the lie that slew you is buried
Under a deeper lie;

But the thing that I saw in your face
No power can disinherit:
No bomb that ever burst
Shatters the crystal spirit.[85]

It suggests a stubborn hope for life and for a voice which can express it. Whether it is bad poetry or good or 'good bad', it succeeds in conveying that conviction.

These themes, together with the sense of truth-telling power that brought them to life in the essay, had to wait till later to be fully explored. In the meantime, it would be hard to think of a better way to prepare for writing a book about them than by following the global power struggle, summarizing its progress week by week, and presenting as much of the best of English literature as possible for a foreign audience.

---

[85] *Works XIII*, p. 511

# A New Vantage Point

## Autumn and Winter 1942

### War poetry

Following his own attempt at it, Orwell made war poetry the subject of 'Voice' for that September. He got Herbert Read to read W. H. Auden's poem 'September 1, 1939', followed by William Empson reading one by George Sutherland Fraser of the 'New Apocalypse' group which made a brief appearance in the 1940s. If those were representative of the time, they show how unrepresentative Orwell's about the Italian militiaman was. They express ambivalence, doubts and fears in complex formulations. Auden, physically safe in America but beleaguered, as he put it, by 'negation and despair,' prays for the ability to 'show an affirming flame'. He sees himself and those with him along a bar in New York as

> Lost in a haunted wood,
> Children afraid of the night
> Who have never been happy or good.[86]

Sutherland, then serving with the army in Egypt, also prays, reflecting on his feeling of weakness:

> Let time forgive me if I fall apart.[87]

Owning up to such states of mind may have sounded refreshingly honest against the braying in the background, but something upbeat was needed as well, so they were followed by a stirring piece of prose, from T. E. Lawrence's *Revolt in the Desert*.[88] Describing the blowing up and ambush of a Turkish troop train by Arab fighters, the reading included the 'terrific roar' of the

---

[86] *Works XIV*, pp. 16-17.

[87] Ibid., p. 18.

[88] Ibid., p. 19. The reader was not designated in the script, and Peter Davison guessed that it was Orwell, but it would have made more sense for the actor Godfrey Kenton to read it, since he was there anyway, to read the last poem, and his voice was strong whereas Orwell's was weak.

explosion, the chatter of machine-guns, 'the furious shower of bullets which stormed along the roofs of the carriages,' sweeping off the soldiers positioned there, and the resolute Lewis gunners leaving the sand littered with the bodies of fleeing Turks. The thrill of successful action contrasted pleasantly with the sense of impotence that had been prevalent on the North Africa front for most of that year in the current war.

Then came Edmund Blunden, still aged only 46 although he seemed already to belong to the vanishing past with the Georgians, reading two of his poems about the First World War, 'Rural Economy' and 'Report on Experience'. Bleak disillusionment about all that hideous destruction was their theme, but they stated it firmly and without complaining.

From there the script makes its way, via a stilted discussion between Empson, Orwell and Anand, to an *enthusiastic* war poem. It was intended to convey the idea, in Orwell's words, 'that war is not merely a disagreeable necessity, but that it is spiritually better than peace – the kind of peace you have in Vichy France, for instance.'

> 'ANAND: What about an example?
> ORWELL: How about "The Isles of Greece"?

ANAND: Of course! That comes very near home nowadays.
ORWELL: Here it is, then. "The Isles of Greece", by Lord Byron.'[89]

Godfrey Kenton, a Shakespearean actor who had joined the BBC for the duration of the war, then read all sixteen of the six-line stanzas. He had 'a beautiful voice with a very distinctive gravity in its tone,'[90] just right to bring the 25-minute programme to a sonorous finale with the words:

A land of slaves shall ne'er be mine –
Dash down yon cup of Samian wine!

Although the readings had covered the spectrum of emotions from abjection to exaltation, Orwell continued his search for effective war poetry till he was rewarded by a surprising find: Thomas Hardy's long verse drama, *The Dynasts*, first published as one book in 1910. The insights it gave him were not the right kind for broadcasting so he wrote about it in *Tribune* instead, warming to 'its grandiose and rather evil vision of armies marching and counter-

---

[89] *Works XIV*, p. 22.

[90] Richard Bebb, 'Obituary: Godfrey Kenton', *Independent*, 15 May 1998.

marching through the mists, and men dying by hundreds of thousands in the Russian snows, and all for absolutely nothing.'[91] The atmosphere of collective insanity prefigured not only that of the current war but *Nineteen Eighty-Four*. 'Of course,' he says of Hardy,

the idea of huge and meaningless suffering appeals deeply to him, and in the form chosen for *The Dynasts* his strange mystical pessimism gets a freer rein than it could get in a novel, where a certain amount of probability is needed. Hardy set free his genius by writing a drama which was definitely not meant to be acted, and quite unknowingly – for *The Dynasts* was written round about 1900 – produced something that would do as it stands for the script of a talkie.[92]

If that was so, Orwell's own 'strange mystical pessimism' might yet find a genre that could give it a free rein. All his novels had suffered from lack of probability, and the realization that some kinds of narrative did not require much of it removed a major obstacle from his path. These thoughts led

[91] Ibid., p. 45.
[92] Ibid., p. 43.

him to the conclusion that 'even a half-lunatic view of life will do as a basis for literature provided it is sincerely held.'[93] For someone who had been at odds with the prevailing view of the world for most of his life and had never belonged to any set, group or clique, this must have been seriously encouraging. He never tried writing 'a script for a talkie', but the following year did adapt stories for radio drama. Heightened awareness of the sound of verbal compositions was enlivening his sensibility both as a reader and as a writer.

## Moving on

If he had been nurturing any hopes of finding an outlet for his powers in radio, they were dashed, according to his diary, at the beginning of October, by a report on the uselessness of all his work:

> Long talk with Brander, who is back after his 6 month tour in India. His conclusions so depressing that I can hardly bring myself to write them down. Briefly, affairs are much worse in India than anyone here is allowed to

[93] Ibid., p. 45.

realise, the situation is in fact retrievable but won't be retrieved because the government is determined to make no real concessions, hell will break loose when and if there is a Japanese invasion, and our broadcasts are utterly useless because nobody listens to them.[94]

Lawrence Brander wrote after the war that this did not diminish Orwell's sense of responsibility, 'for he knew how important radio propaganda could be, if intelligently organized, and he worked very hard on his own talks, which were always good and usually brilliant.'[95] The disheartening news could, however, have reduced any feeling of timidity his responsibilities may have given him. Furthermore, his voice was, according to the Controller of Overseas Services, 'unattractive and really unsuited to the microphone.'[96] No recording of his voice appears to have survived but it was said to be weak because of the damage done to his vocal cords by his bullet wound. This

---

[94] Entry for 5 October 1942, *Diaries*, p. 366.

[95] Lawrence Brander, *George Orwell*. London: Longman, Green, 1954. Cited in *Works XIV*, p. 77.

[96] Clark, J. B. Memo dated 19 January 1943, BBC Archives, http://www.bbc.co.uk/archive/orwell/7438.shtml accessed on 20 July 2011.

disadvantage would have helped him to resist any temptation he might have felt to take up broadcasting as a career. In the meantime, if his work was doing nothing to affect the outcome of the war, he was at least not in danger of doing much harm with it, and could concentrate instead on his own interests.

He went ahead a few days later with a novel-writing experiment he had set up, consisting of five weekly episodes each by a different author, the first one by himself starting: 'It was a night in London in the late autumn of 1940. A bomb came whistling down, piercing the racket of the guns, and a man, a small shadowy figure, darted like a lizard…'[97] One can imagine him taking pleasure in this brief return to his old profession, even if only with the radio equivalent of a passage for a short pot-boiler. When the war had started, he, like other novelists,[98] had felt unable to write another book at such a time, but until then he had still been thinking his next serious work would be

---

[97] Ibid., p. 89.

[98] Storm Jameson, President of the English Centre of International PEN, felt the same way: 'In September 1939 it seemed highly unlikely, as well as slightly indecent, to think of earning a living as a novelist.' In Valerie Holman, *Print for Victory*. London: British Library, 2008, p. 54.

'an enormous novel, a sort of saga (!) which will have to be published in three parts.'[99] Paper shortages, as well as new perspectives and other projects, put paid to that idea.

The other contributors to 'Story by Five Authors' were L. A. G. Strong, Inez Holden, Martin Armstrong and E. M. Forster. The weakest episode was that of Inez Holden, who instead of taking the story forward devoted most of her instalment to the dreams and interior monologue of the main character, who was based on Orwell himself. This may have been because of the intimacy between them. Forster salvaged the project in a masterful way, tying up all the loose ends that had accumulated by the time his turn came. If all the experiment did was steer Orwell away from the idea of writing another novel in the manner of his previous ones, it was well worthwhile.

In a self-portrait written in 1940 for an American dictionary of twentieth century authors,[100] he had numbered T. S. Eliot among the modern writers he cared most about, and the radio

---

[99] In a letter dated 4 July 1939 to his agent, Leonard Moore. *Letters*, p. 169.

[100] Stanley J, Kunitz, H. Haycraft, eds. *Twentieth Century Authors*. New York: Wilson, 1942.

among the things he disliked (along with 'big towns, noise, motor cars, tinned food, central heating and "modern" furniture').[101] By the time the dictionary came out, in 1942, he had learnt to live with the radio and to see Eliot in a sharply critical perspective. The poet, still growing into legendary stature, had published three of his *Four Quartets* by then, and Orwell discussed them in the September-October issue of *Poetry*. He continued to admire the 'wonderful vitality and power' of the earlier work such as *Prufrock*, but that made him all the more critical of 'the gloomy mumblings of these three poems.'[102]

It was 'glowing despair' that gave the early poems their vitality, Orwell thought, and 'melancholy faith' that made the late ones dull:

… the trouble is that conscious futility is something only for the young. One cannot go on 'despairing of life' into ripe old age. One cannot go on and on being 'decadent' since decadence means falling and one can only be said to be falling if one is going to reach the bottom reasonably soon. Sooner or later one is obliged

---

[101] *Collected Essays 2*, p. 40.
[102] *Works XIV*, p. 66.

to adopt a positive attitude towards life and society.[103]

He did not live long enough to witness Samuel Beckett's approach, or to see how a deliberately positive one might wear in the long run. His own experience of that struggle had provided the main subject matter for his novels, *The Clergyman's Daughter* and *Keep the Aspidistra Flying*. Eliot was 54 in 1942, even older than Stafford Cripps. His refuge from despair, as Orwell saw it, was the same as Cripps's, and one he had considered in his down-and-out days for himself: the Anglican Church. Orwell had come to the conclusion that although it offered a kind of support system for a positive attitude, it was at an unacceptable cost:

In theory it is still possible to be an orthodox religious believer without being intellectually crippled in the process, but it is far from easy, and in practice books by orthodox believers usually show the same cramped, blinkered outlook as books by orthodox Stalinists or others who are mentally unfree.'[104]

---

[103] *Works XIV*, p. 65.

[104] Ibid 66.

This view goes with Orwell's opposition to 'all the smelly little orthodoxies which are now contending for our souls,' as he had put it at the end of his essay on Dickens in 1939.[105] There is no obvious hostility in his damning appraisal of Eliot's current work, however, just a conviction that the old master could not be expected to meet present needs.

Eliot would have seen these comments in the October-November issue of *Poetry*, but, unlike H. G. Wells, he remained on civil terms with his lapsed admirer, and accepted his invitation to join the 'Voice' broadcast for December 1. The picture that often goes with Orwell's BBC time shows Eliot sitting at the microphone between J. M. Tambimuttu and Una Marson, with Orwell, smart for once in a dark suit, standing behind, leaning forward to follow the text on the table with a benign smile on his face.[106] The scripts for these discussions seem quaint and ungainly now, but the man who wrote and presented them looks relaxed and intelligent, and the group as a whole lively enough for a genuine pursuit of enlightenment.

---

[105] *Essays 1*, 504.

[106] Several photos of the 'Voice' gatherings have survived, and this one is used in D. J. Taylor's *Orwell – The Life*, between pp. 306 and 307.

By this time Orwell gives the impression of having gone even more native in the sense that he could express his thoughts on the air in a way acceptable to his supervisors as fully as in writing for print or in his diary. This is particularly apparent in 'an imaginary interview' he conducted in November between himself and Jonathan Swift, author of the book which, he said, 'has meant more to me than any other book ever written,'[107] *Gulliver's Travels*. 'There's something in his way of writing that seems to tell you what his voice was like,' he says in the introduction to the interview, so he could have given expert coaching to the reader of Swift's lines.[108] The interview device enabled him here to broadcast some of his favourite opinions, using the words of Swift to express them, some quoted from his works and some pastiche.

On hostility to intelligence: 'When a true Genius appears in the world, you may know him by this infallible sign: that all the *Dunces* are in Confederacy against him.'

---

[107] *Works XIV*, p. 157.

[108] Probably Henry Wickham Steed (ibid., p. 156), who had been Editor of *The Times* from 1919 to 1922.

On progress: 'Whereas previously some petty tyrant was considered to have reached the highest point of human fame if he laid waste a single province and pillaged half a dozen towns [*with ironic pleasure*] your great men nowadays can devastate whole *continents* and condemn entire races of men to slavery.'

On the growth of London: 'Many a green field where Pope and I used to stroll after dinner on Sunday evenings is now a warren of bricks and mortar for the kennelling of Yahoos.'

On smells: 'Tell me candidly,' Orwell asks, 'do we stink as we used to?' Swift answers, 'Certainly the smells are different,' but without offering a view on whether they are any better or worse. Orwell had scandalized readers of *The Road to Wigan Pier* by repeating the Edwardian upper class saying that 'the working classes smell,' and would have been naturally wary of doing it again, but the subject of smells never stopped preoccupying him.

Earlier in his life he had worked at memorizing passages from Swift and writing in his style, which helps to explain the sure-footedness of this piece.[109] A familiar combination of two other features makes it striking as well: its warm reverence for Swift's genius at the beginning of the interview, and its cool dismissal of him at the end:

> He was a great man, and yet he was partially blind. He could only see one thing at a time. His vision of human society is so penetrating, and yet in the last analysis it's false. He couldn't see what the simplest person sees, that life is worth living, and human beings, even if they're dirty and ridiculous, are mostly decent.'[110]

Keeping in view both the strengths and the weaknesses of a given author without 'doublethink' had become Orwell's habitual approach. It was a way to learn from the masters he found congenial without being led astray by their failings. There is a note of sadness in this public parting with his oldest and favourite teacher, as if he felt he was on his own now.

---

[109] A memory of Michael Sayers, Orwell's flat-mate in 1935, told to Gordon Bowker in 2000 (Bowker, p. 176).
[110] *Works XIV*, p. 161.

## However unwillingly, a heroic age

That imagined interview was on Friday 6 November. On Sunday, nine days later, he made the only entry in his diary for that month: 'Church bells rung this morning – in celebration for the victory in Egypt. The first time that I have heard them in over two years.'[111] No one else in England had heard them during that time either (except once because of a false alarm): church-bell-ringing had stopped in 1940 because it was to be the signal that the German invasion had started. This was the last time Orwell wrote in his diary during the war. The habit had perhaps helped him to keep sane and grown-up at the BBC and he could manage without it now. He did not take up diary-writing again till 1946, when he was on the island of Jura, struggling with tuberculosis and *Nineteen Eighty-Four*.

In an article in *Tribune* that December, he laid to rest yet another of his exemplars – the sixth that year, after Kipling, Wells, Dickens, Eliot and Swift. 'No more of any value will come out of Henry Miller,' he announced to open his review of that author's 'latest pot-boiler', *The Colossus of*

---

[111] Diaries, p. 368.

*Maroussi*.[112] And to close it: '*Tropic of Cancer* has its place in the short list of twentieth-century novels that are worth reading.' Giving a surprising twist to his conclusion, he explains the decline of Henry Miller in these terms: 'He was at his best when writing about the unheroic, and we live in what is, however unwillingly, a heroic age.' That age might not have felt heroic if the war had still been going badly, but now the sense of doom had lifted. The Russians were winning in Stalingrad, the Americans were winning in the Pacific, Montgomery had defeated Rommel at the Battle of El Alemein, Allied forces under Eisenhower had landed in Morocco and Algeria. Morale was high for the first time in years, and Orwell apparently could not help having the same collective feeling even if he knew there must be a catch in it.

The 1940s now look heroic as well, in comparison to the times that followed.[113] Orwell himself was a kind of hero to his boss at the BBC, L. F. Rushbrook Williams, who wrote on his

---

[112] 'The End of Henry Miller'. In *Tribune*, 4 December 1942, *Works XIV*, p. 217.

[113] See, for example, Andrew Marr, p. 355: 'Heroism was distributed widely, embracing pensioners and firefighters, air-raid wardens and nursing mothers.'

annual staff report, 'I have the highest opinion of his moral as well as his intellectual capacity. He is transparently honest, incapable of subterfuge, and, in early days, would have been either canonized – or burnt at the stake! Either fate he would have sustained with stoical courage.'[114] Others who admire Orwell do so because he was definitely *not* a saint. He also continues to be condemned by conservatives and socialists alike as a heretic.[115]

Be that as it may, a pleasant sense of virtue rewarded was in the air by the end of the year. Even the weekly news reviews had creative possibilities now, and Orwell used them to have fun examining the German attempts to break bad news in a positive way.

To read the German communiqués of this moment you'd think that retreating was the whole art of war, and certainly some of their phrases are most ingenious. We have all heard

---

[114] L. F. Rushbrook Williams, Annual Confidential Report for E. A. Blair, Eastern Service, 10 August 1943. BBC Archives, accessed at http://www.bbc.co.uk/archive/orwell/7438.shtml on 20 July 2011.

[115] See Hitchens, *Why Orwell Matters*, for an entertaining discussion of the views on offer.

of 'strategic withdrawals' and 'elastic defence' but the German commentators have thought of better ones than that. Their best phrase to describe a rapid retreat is 'We have successfully increased the distance between ourselves and the enemy'; another is 'We have compelled the British to advance westward' – also, of course, that by choosing to retreat General Rommel 'retains the initiative'. You will have noticed that when a dog is chasing a rabbit, the rabbit retains the initiative.[116]

A week later, on Boxing Day, for the last news review of the year, Orwell concluded: 'There have been moments even during 1942 – especially during the middle of the summer – when things looked dark enough, but we can see now with certainty that the tide has turned.'[117]

The last edition of 'Voice' was 'a special Christmas number' which included a recording of *Adeste Fideles* to start with, a reading of the nativity story from the Gospel of St Matthew, a recording of a carol called 'The Seven Joys of Mary,' a recording of T. S. Eliot's 'The Journey

---

[116] News Commentary 52, 19 December, *Works XIV*, p. 243.

[117] News Commentary 53, 26 December, ibid. p. 259.

of the Magi' read by Eliot, and a reading by
Empson of Robert Bridges' 'Christmas Eve
1913'. 'We'll have the poem, and then straight
after it another carol to end up with. We'll have IN
DULCE JUBILO, or as much of it as we've got time
for.'[118] For a taste of the Bridges poem, this is the
middle stanza:

> Now blessed be the tow'rs
> that crown England so fair
> That stand up strong in prayer
> unto God for our souls:
> Blessed be their founders
> (said I) an' our country folk
> Who are ringing for Christ
> in the belfries tonight
> With arms lifted to clutch
> the rattling ropes that race
> Into the dark above
> and the mad romping din.[119]

The programme blended piety with patriotism
in an enjoyably old-fashioned way, with Orwell
benignly presiding. Before the war he had written:

---

[118] 'Voice' 6, 29 December, ibid., p. 268.
[119] Ibid., p. 269.

> A happy vicar I might have been
> Two hundred years ago,
> To preach upon eternal doom
> And watch my walnuts grow;[120]

and now here he was, being just that, albeit briefly, a happy vicar. Neither his own beliefs nor those of the Hindu, Muslim and Buddhist ones of his target audience were allowed to spoil the party. At that point he probably would not have felt that this was all a waste of time.

---

[120] Written in 1935, quoted in 'Why I write', *Decline of the English Murder and Other Essays*. Harmondsworth: Penguin, 1981, p. 185.

# Epilogue

## 1943 and Beyond

For the pleasure of a happy ending we can leave George Orwell there enjoying a rare moment of collective euphoria. In reality of course things don't end like that, and the story of the outcome of his efforts still has not ended. 1942 was also marked by the publication of William Beveridge's *Report on Social and Allied Services* which led to the National Health Service and, on the same day, Wednesday 2 December, Enrico Fermi's achievement of a controlled nuclear chain reaction which led to the nuclear arms race. The possibility of improving the health of everybody and of killing everybody has gone on increasing since then, with no end yet in sight. From Orwell's perspective, if the war was going to end in a triumph for British imperialism allied with

Russian totalitarianism and American capitalism, what hope was there for a world worth living in? Back in the saddle in January 1943, he was already telling his *Partisan Review* readers: 'As to the real moral of the last three years – that the Right has more guts and ability than the Left – no one will face up to it.'[121]

He continued to fulfil his duties conscientiously at the BBC, but no longer having to bust himself to learn the job or try to achieve the impossible to help win the war. The danger of India being invaded receded as Japan lost ground, and winning sympathy for its colonial masters remained impossible, as well as unnecessary, while they were keeping its most popular leaders locked up. The weekly news bulletins could continue in a more relaxed fashion now that the news was mostly cheering, and the emphasis shifted to education programmes. The work of lining up speakers on literary, scientific, religious and philosophical subjects was more administrative than creative, but it did keep him in close touch with the knowledge, opinions and brain-power available at that time.

---

[121] 'A Letter from England' to *Partisan Review*, 3 January 1943. *Works XIV*, p. 293.

In the summer of 1943 he learnt one new broadcasting technique: turning stories into half-hour audio-dramas. He did this for *Crainquebille* by Anatole France, *The Fox* by Ignazio Silone, *A Slip under the Microscope* by H. G. Wells, *The Emperor's New Clothes* of Hans Christian Andersen, and, perhaps most challengingly, *Macbeth*. His versions of all of them were gripping but, perhaps inevitably given their brevity, failed to achieve a sense of completeness. For *Macbeth*, which he rated 'probably the most perfect of Shakespeare's plays,'[122] he narrated the story, adding dramatic readings from selected scenes. His version was a tale of ambition leading through crime to a regime of terror brought down at last by free individuals backed up by an English army. 'All art is propaganda,' he had observed in his 1939 essay on Dickens and again not long after his induction course at the BBC,[123] and by this time the insight has become a deep and liberating one. Here his reading of the most perfect play he could think of comes across as the most perfect piece of propaganda as well, going far beyond strategy and tactics.

---

[122] *Works XV*, p. 280.

[123] 'No, Not One', *Works XIII*, p. 39.

Good at it though he was, the educational broadcasting was a kind of reversion to the school-mastering he had done in his young days to keep bread on the table, and he had never wanted to be a teacher, or any kind of academic, still less a bureaucrat. It was time to move on, and on 24 September 1943 he wrote his resignation letter to Rushbrook Williams. He was not resigning because of any grievance or disagreement with the BBC, he explained, but because he was not achieving anything there. 'I feel that by going back to my normal work of writing and journalism I could be more useful than I am at present.'[124]

He left in November, became an editor and columnist for *Tribune*, and started writing *Animal Farm*. The latter was, he recalled later, 'the first book in which I tried, with full consciousness of what I was doing, to fuse political purpose and artistic purpose into one whole.'[125] His previous three books had been a political memoir (*Homage to Catalonia*, 1938); a novel (*Coming up for Air*, 1939) and a tract (*The Lion and the Unicorn*,

---

[124] *Works XV*, p. 251.

[125] 'Why I write' (1947), in *Decline of the English Murder and Other Essays*. Harmondsworth: Penguin, 1965; p. 187.

1941). The idea of writing both to convince and to enthral simultaneously, both at full strength, had become a reality for him between 1941 and 1943.

Having acquired a more interactive way of writing at the BBC, he continued it at home, reading his day's work on *Animal Farm* to Eileen in bed at night, discussing the plot with her and welcoming her criticisms and suggestions.[126] It is no coincidence that his most flawless book was also the one he wrote in a mode of listening and being listened to.

In 1945 Eileen died under anaesthetic for a hysterectomy, and the loss, together with his own increasing illness from tuberculosis, accounts for some of the darkness of *Nineteen Eighty-Four*. His two-year stint as a functionary, with all the frustrations and absurdities it had entailed, provided most of the imagery for the rest. The canteen, the work spaces, the dreaded Room 101, the social life, the singing cleaning ladies, the air fetid with propaganda and the whole atmosphere of the Ministry of Truth came directly from Broadcasting House. It was a much less perfect book than *Animal Farm* but also much more shocking, with its combination of nightmare and

---

[126] Crick, p. 451.

realistic detail. As a result, it had an even bigger impact. It had sold about 25 million copies by the end of the 20th century, and *Animal Farm* about 20 million.[127] The millions have continued to increase in the 21st, climbing steeply with the rise of 'post-truth' and populist politics. Orwell certainly did embark on something 'more useful', when he left his radio job to start writing in this new way. If he had stayed there much longer he might never have got around to it. That is hypothetical. What we do know is that by the time he left the BBC he had found the way to set free his genius.

---

[127] John Rodden gives the latter figure in *Understanding Animal Farm.* London: Greenwood Press, 1999; p. 120. The former is attributed by Wikipedia to *The Philadelphia Enquirer* of 22 June 2009. Both are fallible but useful for an idea of a probable order of magnitude.

# Bibliography

## By George Orwell

Orwell, George. *Down and Out in Paris and London* (1933). Harmondsworth: Penguin, 1982

*Burmese Days* (1934). Harmondsworth: Penguin, 1983

*A Clergyman's Daughter* (1935). Harmondsworth: Penguin, 1983

*Keep the Aspidistra Flying* (1936). Harmondsworth: Penguin, 1983

*The Road to Wigan Pier* (1937). Harmondsworth: Penguin, 1961

*Homage to Catalonia* (1938). Harmondsworth: Penguin, 1983

*Coming Up for Air* (1939). Harmondsworth: Penguin, 1984

*The Lion and the Unicorn* (1941). London: Secker and Warburg, 1962

*Animal Farm* (1945). Harmondsworth: Penguin, 1989

*Nineteen Eighty-Four* (1949). Harmondsworth: Penguin, 1954

*Decline of the English Murder and Other Essays*. Harmondsworth: Penguin, 1981

*Inside the Whale and Other Essays*. Harmondsworth: Penguin, 1981

Davison, Peter, ed. *The Complete Works of George Orwell* (20 volumes). London: Secker & Warburg, 1998. In particular:

*XIII. All Propaganda is Lies, 1941-1942*

*XIV. Keeping our Little Corner Clean, 1942-1943*

*XV. Two Wasted Years, 1943*

*XVI. I Have Tried to Tell the Truth, 1943-1944*

*George Orwell Diaries*. London: Harvill Secker, 2010

*Orwell: A Life in Letters*. London: Harvill Secker, 2010

Orwell, Sonia, and Angus, Ian, eds. *The Collected Essays, Journalism and Letters of George Orwell*. Harmondsworth: Penguin, 1970. 4 volumes:

## About George Orwell

Bowker, Gordon. *George Orwell.* London: Little Brown, 2003

Brander, Lawrence. *George Orwell*. London: Longman, Green, 1954

Clark, J. B. Memorandum dated 19 January 1943, BBC Archives, accessed at http://www.bbc.co.uk/archive/orwell/7438.shtml on 20 July 2011

Crick, Bernard. *George Orwell: A Life*. London: Penguin, 1980

Coppard, Audrey, and Crick, Bernard, eds. *Orwell Remembered*. London: BBC, 1984

Davison, Peter. 'Two Wasted Years?' *Finlay Publisher – The Orwell Essay*, 2011, January – March, accessed at www.finlay-publisher.com on 12 April 2011

'Orwell: Religious and Ethical Values', *Finlay Publisher – The Orwell Essay*, 2008, March–

May, accessed at www.finaly-publisher.com on 5 July 2011

Hitchens, Christoper. *Why Orwell Matters*. New York: Basic Books, 2002

*Hitch-22*. London: Atlantic, 2011

Rees, Richard. *George Orwell: Fugitive from the Camp of Victory*. Carbondale: Southern Illinois University Press, 1961

Rodden, John, ed. *Understanding Animal Farm*. London: Greenwood Press, 1999

Rushbrook Williams, L. F. 'Annual Confidential Report for E. A. Blair, Eastern Service, 10 August 1943' BBC Archives, accessed at http://www.bbc.co.uk/archive/orwell/7438.shtml on 20 July 2011

Taylor, D. J. *Orwell: The Life*. London: Vintage, 2003

'Orwell's Poetry', *Finlay Publisher – The Orwell Essay*, December 2008 – January 2009, accessed at www.finaly-publisher.com on 5 July 2011

Warburg, Fredrick. *All Authors are Equal*. London: Hutchinson, 1973

Woodcock, George. *The Crystal Spirit*. Harmondsworth: Penguin, 1970

## About the Second World War

Axelrod, Alan. *The Real History of World War II – A New Look at the Past*. New York: Sterling, 2008

Churchill, Winston. *The Hinge of Fate* (1951). London: Penguin, 2005

Clarke, Peter. *The Cripps Version*. London: Penguin, 2002

Holman Valerie. *Print for Victory*. London: British Library, 2008

Marr, Andrew. *The Making of Modern Britain*. London: Macmillan, 2009

Mellersh, H. E. L. et al., eds. *The Hutchinson Chronology of World History*. Oxford: Helicon, 1998

Nicolson, Harold. *Why Britain is at War*. London: Penguin, 1939 and 2010